2/19

AL
HL

Please return/renew this item by the last date shown
on this label, or on your self-service receipt.

To renew this item, visit **www.librarieswest.org.uk**
or contact your library.

Your Borrower Number and PIN are required.

LibrariesWest

Immigration

WORLD ISSUES

Harriet Brundle

BookLife

WORLD ISSUES

©2016
Book Life
King's Lynn
Norfolk PE30 4LS

ISBN: 978-1-78637-022-8

Written by:
Harriet Brundle

Designed by:
Ian McMullen

A catalogue record for this book
is available from the British Library.

Contents

Words that look like *this* can be found in the Glossary on page 30.

Words that look like **this** are key words to remember.

What is an Immigrant?

Key Terms

An **immigrant** is a person who has come to live in another country permanently. When a person leaves the country that they live in they have **emigrated**. While a person is moving between different places, they are **migrating**.

Legal immigrants are people who have been allowed to live and work in a different country by that country's authorities. **Illegal immigrants** have moved to live in a new country without making themselves known to the authorities or have stayed somewhere longer than they were supposed to.

A person is said to be seeking *asylum* when they arrive in a new country and hope that the country's government will offer them protection and allow them to live there. Every person in the world has the right to seek asylum.

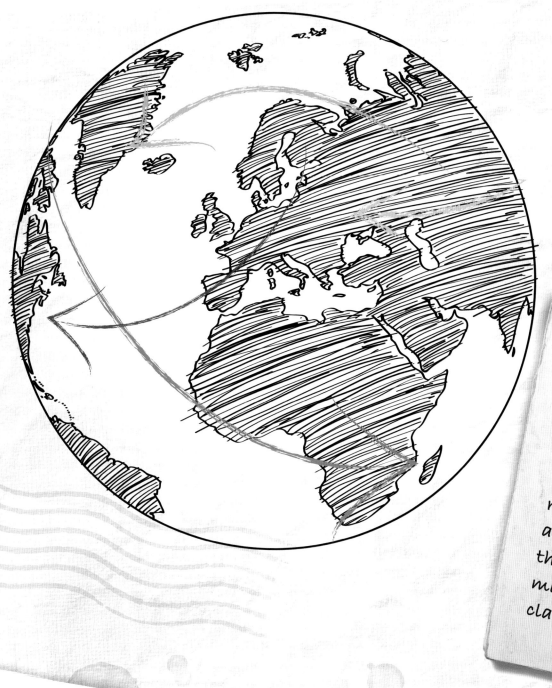

The number of asylum applications in the United Kingdom reached its highest in 2002.

We can find out where migrants are moving to around the world by the asylum applications each country receives. This isn't always accurate though, as many migrants do not claim asylum.

Why do People Emigrate?

There are many different reasons why people emigrate. Those that choose to leave their home country might do so because they want a different job that they can't get where they currently live, they may have the opportunity to earn more money, or they might be moving to be with loved ones who live in a different country.

These reasons are called **pull factors** because they are ones that pull or attract people to move to another country.

141,000 people emigrated from Britain in 2013

139,000 people emigrated from Britain in 2014

Other people leave their country because they need to protect themselves and their families from harm. Their country may be at war or there may have been a **natural disaster**. Their home may have been destroyed or they may not feel safe and so they leave to find a new place to live that they hope will be safer.

These reasons are called *push factors* because they are ones that push or force people to move to another country.

People who have had no choice but to leave their home to protect themselves are called **refugees**.

How do People Migrate?

People who are **migrating** because of **pull factors** may choose to move to their new home by aeroplane or by car. They have usually planned their journey, will take all their belongings with them and will have a new home or place to stay already prepared for them to move into.

PASSPORT

This process can take some time. Some countries have forms that must be completed and approved by authorities before a person can move there to live.

Those that are forced to **migrate** because of **push factors** often have to leave their home unexpectedly. They may not have time to plan their journey or gather up their belongings and they have no choice but to travel to a new country on foot, by boat, in cars and lorries.

The journey can be very dangerous. 71 people were found dead in a lorry in Austria in 2015; it is thought they were refugees from Syria. The lorries have little space and are often sealed so those inside are cut off from fresh air.

Many refugees make the journey to a new home on foot. Refugees have to carry their belongings with them and the journeys can be many miles long. Many people are travelling with family members, including older people and children.

The journeys may be along dangerous routes, including on busy roads. Thousands of refugees have made the journey along the side of the M1 motorway in Hungary, trying to reach the Austrian border. From there, they hope to reach Germany.

100 Miles

The journey taken on foot by refugees from Hungary to Austria is one hundred miles long.

Many refugees and immigrants are attempting to enter countries inside lorries. While the lorries are at a standstill, people climb inside the container areas and hope to hide there until they reach their destination.

For many, they have no choice but to pay large sums of money to people smugglers who then help the refugees and immigrants move to a different country. People smuggling is illegal and is extremely dangerous as the methods used by the smugglers are often unsafe.

Despite the threat of arrest, thousands of people smugglers operate all around the world every day.

Migration *by Boat*

Aegean Sea

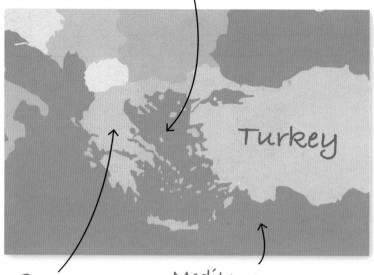

Greece

Mediterranean Sea

For many **refugees**, they have no choice but to travel to a new country by boat. The routes taken include travelling across the **Mediterranean** and **Aegean Seas** from Syria and Turkey to the Greek Islands. If they manage to reach mainland Greece, the refugees hope to travel into countries such as the UK, France and Germany.

Sadly, many migrants do not survive the journey across the sea.

Once the refugees arrive, the Greek Islands are not prepared for the large numbers of people and so cannot find them all a place to stay.

It is estimated that more than 360,000 refugees crossed the Mediterranean Sea in 2015 compared to just 70,000 in 2011.

2011
70,000

2015
360,000

The boats used to make the journey across the water are often small and unsteady fishing boats or flimsy rubber boats that are not suitable for rough seas. The boats are often **overcrowded** and the extra weight puts the small boats under strain, so they often sink or overturn. If lots of people are squashed together, illness can spread very quickly and make people unwell.

Over 300 migrants died in rough Mediterranean seas in one incident alone in February 2015.

Illness can spread quickly when people are crammed on to boats.

13

Refugee Camps

A **refugee camp** is a temporary place for refugees to live, as they cannot stay in their home country because it is too dangerous. The camps are usually set up by a government or a charity, such as the Red Cross.

It is not unusual for thousands of people to be staying in a refugee camp until they find somewhere permanent to live.

As the camps are only meant to be temporary, they are very basic. The camps are overcrowded; there is often not enough food and they can be unclean, which can make people become very unwell.

In 1999, a refugee camp called Sangatte opened in Calais, France, close by to the Channel Tunnel which connects France with England. As a result of it opening, hundreds of refugees flocked to the camp with the hope of reaching England. As well as refugees, the camp also attracted many illegal immigrants who were trying to reach the UK and this made the refugee camp become extremely **controversial**.

Calais

England

France

The number of people staying at the camp was far more than expected and so the camp became overcrowded and unclean.

When the camp was finally closed in 2002 by the then President of France Nicolas Sarkozy, there were **riots**. Today, many migrants live in camps in Calais hoping to cross into England.

How Does it Feel to be an Immigrant?

For immigrants who are moving because of pull factors, the journey to a new place can be exciting. They may be looking forward to seeing loved ones or seeing their new home for the first time.

How would you feel if you were moving to a new home? Why do you think you would feel like that?

It can be a sad time for immigrants. They might miss their old home, or friends and other family members that may not have moved with them.

When people migrate for a better job so they can earn more money, it is called *economic migration*.

16

For refugees, the journey to a new home can be frightening. They have had to leave their home and perhaps members of their families, with only the belongings they had time to gather and could carry.

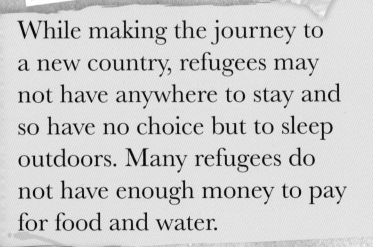

While making the journey to a new country, refugees may not have anywhere to stay and so have no choice but to sleep outdoors. Many refugees do not have enough money to pay for food and water.

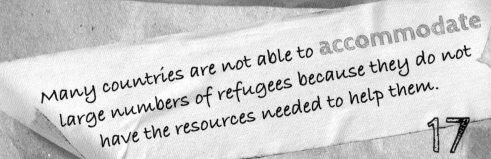

Many countries are not able to accommodate large numbers of refugees because they do not have the resources needed to help them.

How Does it Feel to Live in a New Country?

When immigrants arrive in a new country, it can be very difficult to begin with. They may have gone to a country where people speak a different language and so they cannot understand what others are saying. This is called a **language barrier**.

Think about how frustrating this would be in day-to-day life. Doing simple tasks, for example asking for help in a shop or reading road signs would become very difficult.

A language barrier can also make it difficult to make new friends.

There may be other things that immigrants are not used to in a new country, such as food they may not previously have eaten and different styles of clothing. These are called *cultural differences*.

Many immigrants may want to wear a style of clothing that is traditional within their religion or home country; however, these clothes may look very different to the clothing worn in a new country.

For many immigrants, these differences may make it more difficult for them to feel as though they fit in.

19

How do Others Feel About Immigration?

Many governments throughout the world have different ideas on how best to help refugees. Other people may feel that their country should help larger numbers of refugees; others feel that their country does not have the resources to be able to help and therefore, the number of immigrants and refugees allowed to enter should be limited.

For the last twenty years, the United Kingdom has had a larger number of people immigrating than people emigrating. The difference between the two is called **net migration**.

REFGEES
← WELCOME

Another opinion is that immigrants who travel to new countries because of pull factors help to bring new skills into a country. Immigrants who are skilled in a profession, for example a doctor or dentist, are able to do jobs that the country may not previously have had enough professionals to do.

Many immigrants are healthy and are able to work. When at work, they pay taxes which help to fund public services, which includes the police force and the army.

Some countries measure a person's skills in points, to decide if they should be allowed into the country. Find out more about this on page 23.

Immigration *Laws*

The European Union (EU) is made up of twenty-eight different European countries. One member of government from each of the countries makes up the **European Council**. The council meet at least four times a year in Brussels to make decisions on important issues that affect the countries in Europe.

Each of the countries in the EU have both EU laws and their own national laws.

The EU introduced the **freedom of movement act**, which meant that people living in the twenty-eight EU countries had permission to move freely to any other EU country. As a result, the number of immigrants in Europe has increased.

Other places are more difficult to move to. Some countries, such as Australia, have a points system; each person must have enough points to be allowed to live there. This is called the *General Skilled Migration* points system.

If you do not score enough points, you cannot apply to live in Australia.

A person gets points for lots of different things, including how well they can speak English, what job they do and the skills this gives them, their level of education and their age.

Immigration: *Timeline*

**Migration has been happening since the beginning of time.
All around the world, people are moving to a new home every day.
This timeline shows some events through recent history that have
caused large amounts of people to move to a new place.**

The Empire Windrush

A boat, called the Empire Windrush, arrived
in the United Kingdom carrying migrants
from the Caribbean. This was the start of
mass migration from the Caribbean into
the United Kingdom.

1849   1948

The Irish Potato Famine

When the potato crop failed, many
Irish people emigrated from Ireland
and moved to live in other countries,
such as England, America and Canada.

War in Afghanistan

Millions of people left their home in Afghanistan during the war. Many of the refugees went to countries close to Afghanistan, like Pakistan and Iran.

War in Syria Began

Over four million Syrian refugees have left their home in Syria since 2011 because of war. The refugees are travelling across land and sea to reach countries they hope will be safer.

2001

2004

Freedom of Movement

This act, put in place by the EU, meant that people living in any of the countries that are part of the EU could move freely to any other of these countries.

2011

Case Study: Iraq

Iraq is a country in the Middle East, located next to Turkey, Syria and Iran. The capital of Iraq is called Baghdad. People who are from Iraq are called Iraqi.

In 2003, America invaded Iraq and following this, the people of Iraq suffered many years of war. Every family in Iraq has been affected by the ongoing war. Over two million Iraqi people have been forced to leave their home because of the violence.

Many Iraqi refugees emigrated to countries such as America and the United Kingdom.

Syria

Iraq

Jordan

Other refugees emigrated to nearby countries; nearly one million Iraqis emigrated into Syria and Jordan. Unfortunately, these countries were not able to accommodate such large numbers and as a result, life in their new country has been extremely difficult for the refugees.

America is now working with Iraq, and some American army troops have stayed in Iraq with the hope of making the country safer for the Iraqi people.

Many refugees were unable to find somewhere to stay, buy food or find clean water to drink. Many were also separated from their families.

27

Activities

Each of these key terms has a matching definition in the list below. Can you match up each word with the correct definition?

Immigrant

Emigrate

Migrant

Refugee

Push Factors

Pull Factors

Language Barrier

A person who is moving between different places

Two people that speak different languages and so cannot understand what the other is saying

Reasons such as war or natural disaster that force a person to leave their home country

A person who cannot live in their home country anymore because it is too dangerous

Reasons such as a new job that make people want to move to a new country

To leave your home country

A person who has come to live in another country permanently

Write a letter to a pen pal who is moving to your home country.

Think about all the things you can tell them about where you live. What language do you speak? What sort of weather can they expect? What food do you eat that you could tell them about? Where do you go to school?

Glossary

Accommodate – to offer shelter and help

Authorities – a person/group with the right to make decisions and give orders

Basic – simple

Belongings – things that belong to a person

Controversial – something that causes public disagreement

Definition – the meaning of a word

European – anything about the continent of Europe

Limited – when something has limits or is stopped at a set amount

Mass – lots of

Natural Disaster – a natural event, such as an earthquake, that causes great damage or loss of life

Overcrowded – too many people

Permanently – something that lasts forever

Riots – a violent reaction from a crowd of people

Temporary – when something lasts for a short amount of time

Smugglers – people who take other people to a new place secretly and usually illegally

Index

Photo Credits

WORLD
ISSUES